¡Las mascotas son geniales!
Pets Are Awesome!

MI GATO
MY CAT

Norman D. Graubart
Traducción al español: Christina Green

PowerKiDS press™

New York

For Annie, Hey, and Buckley

Published in 2014 by The Rosen Publishing Group, Inc.
29 East 21st Street, New York, NY 10010

First Edition

Book Design: Colleen Bialecki
Photo Research: Katie Stryker

Traducción al español: Christina Green

Photo Credits: Cover Schubbel/Shutterstock.com; p. 5 Noam Armonn/Shutterstock.com; p. 7 Ekaterina Cherkashina/ Shutterstock.com; p. 9 borzywoj/Shutterstock.com; p. 11 Dan Kosmayer/Shutterstock.com; p. 13 MJTH/ Shutterstock.com; p. 15 Anastasija Popova/Shutterstock.com; p. 17 Joyce Vincent/Shutterstock.com; p. 19 Fer Gregory/Shutterstock.com; p. 21 Krissi Lundgren/Shutterstock.com; p. 23 Oria/Shutterstock.com.

Library of Congress Cataloging-in-Publication Data

Graubart, Norman D.
 My cat = Mi gato / by Norman D. Graubart ; translated by Christina Green. — First edition.
    pages cm. — (Pets are awesome! = ¡Las mascotas son geniales!)
English and Spanish.
Includes index.
ISBN 978-1-4777-3304-2 (library)
1. Cats—Juvenile literature. I. Green, Christina, translator. II. Graubart, Norman D. My cat. III. Graubart, Norman D. My cat. Spanish. IV. Title. V. Title: Mi gato.
 SF445.7.G7318 2014
 636.8–dc23
                                                        2013022455

Web Sites: Due to the changing nature of Internet links, PowerKids Press has developed an online list of Web sites related to the subject of this book. This site is updated regularly. Please use this link to access the list: www.powerkidslinks.com/paa/cat/

Manufactured in the United States of America

CPSIA Compliance Information: Batch # W14PK3: For Further Information contact Rosen Publishing, New York, New York at 1-800-237-9932

CONTENIDO

CONTENTS

Los gatos son mascotas adorables. Son la segunda mascota más popular de los Estados Unidos.

Cats are cute pets. They are the second-most-popular pets in the United States.

Todos los gatos bebé nacen con los ojos azules.
Muchos gatos cambian de color de ojos a medida que crecen.

All kittens are born with blue eyes. Many cats' eyes change color as they get older.

Los gatos tienen bigotes. Los bigotes les ayudan a sentir el piso por el que caminan de noche.

Cats have whiskers. Whiskers help cats feel the ground at night.

9

Hay muchas razas diferentes de gatos. El gato elfo es una mezcla del *curl* americano y del gato esfinge.

There are many different breeds of cats. The elf cat is a mix of the American curl cat and the sphynx cat.

Un gato con rayas o manchas se llama *tabby* o **atigrado**.

A cat with stripes or spots is called a **tabby**.

A una mamá gato también
se la llama reina.

A mother cat is called
a queen.

Los gatos se limpian lamiéndose el cuerpo. Esto se llama **acicalarse**.

Cats clean themselves by licking their bodies. This is called **grooming**.

Los gatos son buenos cazadores.

Cats are good hunters.

La raza singapura es la más pequeña.

The Singapura is the smallest breed.

21

A muchas personas les gustan los gatos. ¡Si amas a tu gato, él te amará también!

Lots of people love cats. If you love your cat, it will love you, too!

23

PALABRAS QUE DEBES SABER
WORDS TO KNOW

acicalarse
grooming

atigrado
tabby

(los) bigotes
whiskers

ÍNDICE

INDEX